WHEN THE HEAVENS SEEM **CLOSED** | JOSH PENNINGTON

CONTENTS

ACKNOWLEDGMENTS

To my wife, Angie, for her never-ending love and support. I love you more than words, and I am deeply grateful we get to share this life.

To my children, Julia, Jacob, Lauren, Audrey, and Alex, whose insistence gave me the courage to put my thoughts on paper. Thank you for believing in me. I love you all to the moon and back.

To Janet Loos for your creativity and kindness, which made this project come alive.

To Alexandra Scarsella for going above and beyond and getting this book back on track.

DEDICATION

It is only fitting that the one who gave me life gets the credit for my first published work, my mother. The heart and soul of this book belong to her. She helped me in more ways than I can express. She left too soon. I trust this honors her life and memory. I wish she could have seen this with her own eyes. Somehow, I feel like she can. I dedicate this book to my mom.

PREFACE

This book contains my thoughts following a series of messages I preached in late 2011, shortly after my mom passed away. I have struggled with this project for several reasons. First, it brought back the pain. Second, I am not a professionally trained writer—or anything else, for that matter. I am also not the same version of me who delivered these messages. As I read my words, I spent a great deal of time overthinking and wanting to rewrite so many things.

Ultimately, I released the book after realizing this doesn't have to be the best or the last thing I ever say about this subject. It may not sound like much to you, but publishing these thoughts is massive to me. Putting my thoughts out into the world is one of my worst nightmares, but I'm doing it anyway. Not for me, but for you and any other reader who needs this message.

A million thanks for investing your time in reading this project. It came from the heart, and I trust you will feel that as you read.

I hope this book helps you and makes a difference in your life.

INTRODUCTION

What you are about to read was born out of my deepest moments of pain. I have put my entire heart and soul into this book—for you. My simple prayer is that God will use this project to encourage you and breathe hope into your world. All pain has a purpose, and it should never be wasted. I am choosing not to waste my pain. I want to use it as a forensic tool that allows me to navigate through waters that are only seen in dark moments. Rather than your staying stuck in the dark waters of your pain, I believe God will bring you into the multidimensional richness of His unwavering love and grace. I pray that you would find freedom reading these words and seeking Him and His ways.

Whenever I share things that may be personal for me (which I do from time to time in both speaking and writing), I go through a process that enables me to get to a full and complete "yes." You can easily understand or at least acknowledge the possibility of there being some hesitation in my approach to any opportunity to share my thoughts and feelings, especially when judgment, criticism, or misunderstanding could follow. It took me over five years to say "yes" to this book project. Because of the personal nature of the content, it was important that nothing be off-limits. I knew I needed to share every feeling; every emotion; every doubt; every up and down. Every color of the emotional spectrum had to be on the table for my words to be authentic. From the onset, I want you, the reader, to know how important you are to me even though we may never meet in person. It is imperative that I be totally open and vulnerable with you.

I AM NOT SUPPOSED TO TELL YOU THIS

First, I am never 100 percent sure I have learned everything necessary to communicate things that are meaningful and valuable to others. That in itself creates hesitancy in me to open up, to share, to be completely unguarded with my thoughts and ideas. Second, I often wonder, and even worry about, whether my story and the way I articulate it will be captivating enough to grab and then keep your attention. My mind is constantly bombarded with the belief there is certainly someone worse off, with a better story to tell and a better way of telling it than me. That reality sets me on edge and makes me a bit insecure. Lastly, I never want to have the attitude that I have all the answers. I am confident you have at least one relationship with a person who is a know-it-all. (That is not my favorite type of relationship!) I don't have all the answers; I simply have questions, just like you. One of the greatest lessons I learned from my mom is that when I have questions, God has answers!

> **AND ELIJAH THE TISHBITE, OF THE INHABITANTS OF GILEAD, SAID TO AHAB, "AS THE LORD GOD OF ISRAEL LIVES, BEFORE WHOM I STAND, THERE SHALL NOT BE DEW NOR RAIN THESE YEARS, EXCEPT AT MY WORD." THEN THE WORD OF THE LORD CAME TO HIM, SAYING, "GET AWAY FROM HERE AND TURN EASTWARD, AND**

HIDE BY THE BROOK CHERITH, WHICH FLOWS INTO THE JORDAN. AND IT WILL BE THAT YOU SHALL DRINK FROM THE BROOK, AND I HAVE COMMANDED THE RAVENS TO FEED YOU THERE." SO HE WENT AND DID ACCORDING TO THE WORD OF THE LORD, FOR HE WENT AND STAYED BY THE BROOK CHERITH, WHICH FLOWS INTO THE JORDAN. THE RAVENS BROUGHT HIM BREAD AND MEAT IN THE MORNING, AND BREAD AND MEAT IN THE EVENING; AND HE DRANK FROM THE BROOK. AND IT HAPPENED AFTER A WHILE THAT THE BROOK DRIED UP, BECAUSE THERE HAD BEEN NO RAIN IN THE LAND.

—1 KINGS 17:1–7

A METAPHOR

These verses act as a metaphor or a picture, at least in my mind, of how we deal with life when things become challenging and arduous. Maybe the dried-up brook that you are beside right now is marital or relational. Perhaps a relationship that was so full of life, exploding with energy and bursting forth with hope, has just dried up. Perhaps it's a financial brook that has dried up; money that had always flowed freely is now on lockdown, and your bank account is utterly dry. Perhaps it is a physical issue, and healing is what you have been seeking, but the brook of healing has seemingly dried up.

What do you do when you get to a place where you have pushed every button? Pulled every lever? Said every prayer? What happens when it seems as though the answer comes back "no"? If you've been pouring your heart out to God and there appears to be no reply, you may be tired and worn out. If you are having a "dry brook moment," this book is for you. When you decide you are willing to accept that, it will lead you to ask some questions.

Having questions is okay. God is fine with it. He isn't intimidated, rattled, or angered by your questions or mine. Throughout this book, I will voice some of the most personal issues I have ever processed with God. Many of my thoughts and questions emerged out of deep pain, and some of what I say may shock you. But I am going to simply be transparent, knowing in advance that you may judge and criticize. You may be disappointed in some of the questions that I have asked myself and God. But will you stay with me and do something? Will you give your entire self for the three parts of this book and withhold judgment until you reach the final word on the last page? Will you make the commitment to stay engaged until the very end? I want you to engage. I want you not only to read the words on the page, but to truly desire to hear what I am saying. I believe that as you launch into this, God's presence and His Spirit will speak to your heart in the exact way that you need Him to speak to you. I may not cover the particular subject you are hoping to read about, but I believe this: We serve an all-knowing, all-present, all-powerful God who can reach into your situation and circumstances whether I bring it up or not. Let's do that together.

MIRACLE MINDSET

Toward the end of my mom's battle with stage four melanoma, it became increasingly evident that only a miracle would keep her with us. That miracle never came. I am sincerely not bitter about that anymore. Oh, believe me, I was very bitter at the time. I definitely was. (In Part 02 I will unpack this more fully.) In case you don't get to that part, though, you should know something about the "miracle mindset," because you may think that a miracle is a MUST, but maybe it isn't. When the situation calls for the miraculous, and no miracle comes, I submit to you that at that point in time, right then and there, the believer is given the opportunity to occupy the position he or she was born to occupy. That place says that no matter what happens in this life, even if the brook dries up and stays dry, you do not have to surrender your hope. The One who loves you and died for you caused everything that would happen in your future to be filled with undeniable hope, regardless of the outcome in this lifetime. Your hope does not lie in this life here on earth. It doesn't lie in what happens to you here and now. That is not where your hope is to be placed. Your hope is to be firmly planted in what Christ has already done for you. Whether the miracle comes or not. Whether the situation changes or not. Whether it turns out the way you wanted or not.

This is something that every human being will experience. Everyone. No one is exempt. Brooks dry up. It is that simple. I don't want you going through life living from one delusion to the next with this "miracle mindset." We are to live in such a way that no matter what we experience—whether disaster or fortune, jolt or joy, tragedy or triumph—nothing is strong enough to cause us to cast aside the most powerful spiritual components we have at our disposal: faith, hope, and love.

May you never lose hope in the One in whom our eternal hope rests even *When the Heavens Seem Closed.*

PART 01

THE BROOK DRIED UP

DRY DOESN'T MEAN EMPTY

Many people have had the experience of going to church and having someone talk at them. I don't really find that too helpful, for someone to talk at me. I would prefer that someone talk with me, speaking in a way I can understand and then grasp. I will endeavor to do that for you, but before we do that, I'm going to preface everything with this: Whenever I share things that are especially personal for me, which I do from time to time, I go through a process of asking myself questions. If you're anything like me, and if your assignment has ever been to share things that are personal, you must acknowledge the possibility of some hesitation and reservation in your approach. Those opportunities to share your thoughts and feelings, especially if you're not really that good at it, can be intimidating. I don't feel like I'm good at sharing my feelings all the time, and so when I do so, there are questions I ask myself. I'm never a hundred percent sure that I've learned everything I need to learn to communicate things that are meaningful and valuable to others, and so that, all by itself, creates hesitancy in me to open up and be unguarded with my thoughts and ideas.

Second, I often wonder if my story, and the way I communicate it, is captivating enough to keep someone's attention. I realize that certainly there's someone worse off with a better story and a better way of telling their story than I have. That sets me a bit on edge and makes me concerned when I share. Also, because some of the things I'm going to share with you have to do with my mother's death, I'm concerned that because this one event has been important to me, and significant to me, that I'm oversharing or boring individuals with unnecessary repetition. I don't want to be the guy who tells the same story at every party he attends after you've already heard it thirty times. You could be thinking, *Dude, you need a new story to tell because this one is old and washed up. Find something else to say or just don't say anything at all.* I don't want to be that guy!

Finally, I never want to have the attitude that I have all the answers. We all have relationships with people who are know-it-alls. The point in what I want to share is not that I have all the answers, but simply that you may have questions and that's okay. I'm going to voice some questions that I've had throughout the journey. Some of the questions may shock you because certainly you may not think that a person like me, whatever that means, would ever struggle with this idea in life. I know we all have preconceived ideas about a role that a person has, whether they're a manager of an organization or a pastor or a church leader. We sometimes think, *I have these questions, but they would never ask that question. They would never have this problem.* And I'm simply going to be transparent and open, knowing in advance that some people will judge and criticize and be disappointed in some of the questions that I have asked of myself. But that will be a very small number of people. And this book is for the larger number of you who will hear what is being said. I listen, learn, endeavor to grow, and endeavor to find answers. I hope you will too!

The best way of going at this is to tell you how I've walked through this process of asking questions and how I've endeavored to answer those questions. We're going to read some Scriptures together. I'm going to ask you to engage the Scriptures and allow them to engage you. I'm going to ask you not to fall off into a daydream or a distant stare. I'm going to ask you to remain focused and let the Word of God speak to you. And maybe, just maybe, we'll get to some questions that you've asked yourself. I believe that as we launch ourselves into God's presence, God's Spirit will speak to each and every one of our hearts in the exact arena where we need Him to speak. I may not cover your particular questions, but I believe that we serve an all-knowing, all-present, all-powerful God who can reach into your situation and circumstances.

First Kings 17, starting in verse 1, says this:

> AND ELIJAH THE TISHBITE, OF THE INHABITANTS OF GILEAD, SAID TO AHAB, "AS THE LORD GOD OF ISRAEL LIVES, BEFORE WHOM I STAND, THERE SHALL NOT BE DEW NOR RAIN THESE YEARS, EXCEPT AT MY WORD." THEN THE WORD OF THE LORD CAME TO HIM, SAYING, "GET AWAY FROM HERE AND TURN EASTWARD, AND HIDE BY THE BROOK CHERITH, WHICH FLOWS INTO THE JORDAN. AND IT WILL BE THAT YOU SHALL DRINK FROM THE BROOK, AND I HAVE COMMANDED THE RAVENS TO FEED YOU THERE." SO HE WENT AND DID ACCORDING TO THE WORD OF THE LORD, FOR HE WENT AND STAYED BY THE BROOK CHERITH, WHICH FLOWS INTO THE JORDAN. THE RAVENS BROUGHT

HIM BREAD AND MEAT IN THE MORNING, AND BREAD AND MEAT IN THE EVENING; AND HE DRANK FROM THE BROOK. AND IT HAPPENED AFTER A WHILE THAT THE BROOK DRIED UP, BECAUSE THERE HAD BEEN NO RAIN IN THE LAND.

Why did God send him to a place that God knew would dry up? This story paints an amazing picture and gives language to what people go through in their difficult moments. Elijah declared there was going to be no rain. God sent him to a place where he would be provided for, and God provided, as He always does. But the thing that's interesting to me is that the brook, where he was sent, dried up. Put yourself in Elijah's position for just a moment and try to bring it into our modern-day kind of thinking. This is meant to be a metaphor, or a picture, of how we deal with life when things seem to dry up and become challenging and difficult.

Maybe the brook where you are right now, that seems to be

dried up, is one of marital or relational challenges. Perhaps it seems as though that relationship that was so full of life and bursting full of energy and hope has just dried up. Perhaps it's a financial river that has dried up, and your finances have seemed to lock down and dry up. I've talked to so many people in our church family who are experiencing this; they're losing their jobs or they're having to go get extra jobs because it seems as though there is financial dryness in the world around them. Perhaps it is an issue of physical healing that you need. It seems as though you've been pouring your heart out to God with no reply, no response.

What do we do when we get to the place where we've pushed every button, pulled every lever, and said every prayer that we know to pray, and it seems as though no answer comes. When it seems that the brook is dry, I can only share from my experience on this. My experience of going through this sickness with my mom and my family caused me to ask some questions. It caused me to question my faith.

Now, before you freak out and think, *Oh my gosh, the preacher doesn't believe in God anymore.* No, I have not abandoned my faith. But I did come to the place of an examination of what I believed. And when you come to this dry brook moment, when you decide and are willing to accept that sometimes a life has dried up, it will lead you to ask some questions.

Now, let me explain to you a bit about my background. The Bible school training that I received was something like this. There was a great emphasis on faith, and it seemed the resounding idea in theology was, that if you'd only believe, if you just had enough faith, then you would never go through any dry spells. And if you did go through those times, if you did go through a situation that you don't understand and can't explain, and you didn't seem to be getting the results that you intend on getting, or that you desire to get, there must be something wrong *with you*. There must be something you're doing wrong to cause the river to dry up. There must be a lack of faith on your end. Please hear me, this was not what was taught. It was how my pain interpreted what I had heard.

These thoughts bombarded me all throughout my mom's illness. "Man, Josh, if you'd just said the right confessions, if you'd just prayed the right prayer, if you'd just pulled the right lever and pushed the right buttons, then all of a sudden, it would just be like you put the dollar in the vending machine and pushed the button, and eventually your candy bar will come out." Listen, I believe that God is good, and I will not change my belief because my experience doesn't *seem* to line up with what God's Word says, but neither will I allow anyone to speak to me in a tone of voice that implies there's something wrong with me because I am going through a dry season.

If you're going through a dry season as well, God is not angry with you. God's anger and justice was satisfied in the sacrifice of the man Christ Jesus. The Bible says that there is nothing that can separate us from the love of God. But the reality is that we all go through difficult times. And I want to talk about this issue and the role of faith in difficult times. First Corinthians 13:11, says this:

> **WHEN I WAS A CHILD, I SPOKE AS A CHILD, I UNDERSTOOD AS A CHILD, I THOUGHT AS A CHILD; BUT WHEN I BECAME A MAN, I PUT AWAY CHILDISH THINGS. FOR NOW WE SEE IN A MIRROR, DIMLY, BUT THEN FACE TO FACE. NOW I KNOW IN PART, BUT THEN I SHALL KNOW JUST AS I ALSO AM KNOWN. AND NOW ABIDE FAITH, HOPE, LOVE, THESE THREE; BUT THE GREATEST OF THESE IS LOVE.**

Paul was saying that we don't know everything. When we look in the mirror, we're going to see some things we don't like, and it's going to be dark and dim to us. We're not going to understand, but he says that if we just keep growing, if we just keep moving forward, if we just keep learning, if we just keep on seeking God, more and more will be opened to us.

This idea of faith as an escape from all our woes and troubles really vexed me. I lost countless hours of sleep asking God, "Why are we not getting the results that we want to get? What am I doing that is so wrong?" I believe that for countless people, the idea that all you need is a little more faith, that all you need is to speak the right confession and do this next right thing, has done so much harm and damage that these people now question their faith. "If I didn't have enough faith for this, then how will I have enough faith for that?"

I came across an interesting passage of Scripture that talks about faith. Maybe you've read it before. Hebrews 11 is an amazing chapter that lists the conquests of faith. We're going to look at the end of this chapter, because I think it's the less-examined, less-focused-on portion of Scripture from that text. I think we need to look at it because I believe it will help us.

Whether or not you have faith does not determine whether you will go through challenges. Here's what determines that: If you have breath and oxygen in your lungs, then you will go through challenges in this life. And I believe that part of the courageous, powerful Gospel message is that we can understand we're going through challenges in this life and face them head-on with a God who loves us and who will help us through every situation we encounter. Let's look at Hebrews 11:30–40:

> **BY FAITH THE WALLS OF JERICHO FELL DOWN AFTER THEY WERE ENCIRCLED FOR SEVEN DAYS. BY FAITH**

THE HARLOT RAHAB DID NOT PERISH WITH THOSE WHO DID NOT BELIEVE, WHEN SHE HAD RECEIVED THE SPIES WITH PEACE. AND WHAT MORE SHALL I SAY? FOR THE TIME WOULD FAIL ME TO TELL OF GIDEON AND BARAK AND SAMSON AND JEPHTHAH, ALSO OF DAVID AND SAMUEL AND THE PROPHETS: WHO THROUGH FAITH SUBDUED KINGDOMS, WORKED RIGHTEOUSNESS, OBTAINED PROMISES, STOPPED THE MOUTHS OF LIONS, QUENCHED THE VIOLENCE OF FIRE, ESCAPED THE EDGE OF THE SWORD, OUT OF WEAKNESS WERE MADE STRONG, BECAME VALIANT IN BATTLE, TURNED TO FLIGHT THE ARMIES OF THE ALIENS. WOMEN RECEIVED THEIR DEAD RAISED TO LIFE AGAIN. OTHERS WERE TORTURED, NOT ACCEPTING DELIVERANCE, THAT THEY MIGHT OBTAIN A BETTER RESURRECTION. STILL OTHERS HAD TRIAL OF MOCKINGS AND SCOURGINGS, YES, AND OF CHAINS AND IMPRISONMENT. THEY WERE STONED, THEY WERE SAWN IN TWO, WERE TEMPTED, WERE SLAIN WITH THE SWORD. THEY WANDERED ABOUT

IN SHEEPSKINS AND GOATSKINS, BEING DESTITUTE, AFFLICTED, TORMENTED—OF WHOM THE WORLD WAS NOT WORTHY. THEY WANDERED IN DESERTS AND MOUNTAINS, IN DENS AND CAVES OF THE EARTH. AND ALL THESE, HAVING OBTAINED A GOOD TESTIMONY THROUGH FAITH, DID NOT RECEIVE THE PROMISE, GOD HAVING PROVIDED SOMETHING BETTER FOR US, THAT THEY SHOULD NOT BE MADE PERFECT APART FROM US.

All these individuals, with real and living faith in their hearts, experienced very different things—some amazing things and some challenging things. If you believe that faith will cause you to escape from every challenge and every woe, you will live life filled with disappointment. You will have a growing anxiety in your heart toward God. You will have a disgruntled approach to life, and eventually you will become disenfranchised from Him altogether. If you think that faith in Christ is only a tool to escape from hardship, you're only seeing part of the picture.

Faith is not only about escaping from hardship. Faith is about how we *walk through* the hardship, how we *walk through* the difficulty, how we *endure* the pain and the suffering that comes in this life. Faith is not a get-out-of-jail-free card. It is the way we live out our lives. It's how we breathe. It's how we walk. It's how we talk. If only the individuals with faith experience relief from their distress, what do we do with this list of godly people of whom the writer of Hebrews speaks?

If it is the display of faith and only the display of faith that causes us to be redeemed from challenging situations, then what do we do? What can I do with my mom's situation? What do you do with your situation? When difficulty and challenges arise, we embrace what life deals to us, and we keep marching forward. We keep influencing. We keep affecting change. We keep inspiring. We keep encouraging. We keep helping. We don't play the "woe is me" card, claiming, "I'm distressed, and everything's wrong with me. Everyone needs to work to fix me." No, faith is an action that will cause an individual to step outside of themselves and do things no one thought they could do.

Watching my mom suffer in pain was extremely difficult to do. And then to see her in that bed, in the hospital or at home, and hear her say, "Josh, let's put on some music and worship God. Let's pray together," to have her pray over me and prophesy and speak life over me—that is the kind of legacy of faith I'm after. That is the kind of legacy that we as a church should pursue with passion. We don't want to just walk through life, keeping our fingers crossed, hoping everything just turns out right. Sometimes that's how we as Christians approach life, with our fingers crossed hoping nothing goes wrong. And if something does go wrong, then we lose all hope. We lose all heart. And we start asking ourselves questions like the ones I asked. As a child, I thought like a child, but God was able to help me take one step of growth. He allowed me to see my mom lift her hand to worship and magnify the King of Glory. What an amazing testimony of faith!

What an amazing life we can look forward to living, knowing that as Paul said, "in all things, we are more than conquerors through Christ, who loved us and gave Himself for us." Do we really believe that? I think it would be arrogant to say we all believe that in 100 percent of its potential, but I think that we can each take a step and grow.

Let's look at 1 Kings 17, starting in verse 8. When the brook dries up, when the heavens seem closed, what do we do?

> **THEN THE WORD OF THE LORD CAME TO HIM, SAYING, "ARISE, GO TO ZAREPHATH, WHICH BELONGS TO SIDON, AND DWELL THERE. SEE, I HAVE COMMANDED**

A WIDOW THERE TO PROVIDE FOR YOU." SO HE AROSE AND WENT TO ZAREPHATH.

AND WHEN HE CAME TO THE GATE OF THE CITY, INDEED A WIDOW WAS THERE GATHERING STICKS. AND HE CALLED TO HER AND SAID, "PLEASE BRING ME A LITTLE WATER IN A CUP, THAT I MAY DRINK." AND AS SHE WAS GOING TO GET IT, HE CALLED TO HER AND SAID, "PLEASE BRING ME A MORSEL OF BREAD IN YOUR HAND." SO SHE SAID, "AS THE LORD YOUR GOD LIVES, I DO NOT HAVE BREAD, ONLY A HANDFUL OF FLOUR IN A BIN, AND A LITTLE OIL IN A JAR; AND SEE, I AM GATHERING A COUPLE OF STICKS THAT I MAY GO IN AND PREPARE IT FOR MYSELF AND MY SON, THAT WE MAY EAT IT, AND DIE." AND ELIJAH SAID TO HER, "DO NOT FEAR; GO AND DO AS YOU HAVE SAID, BUT MAKE ME A SMALL CAKE FROM IT FIRST, AND BRING IT TO ME; AND AFTERWARD MAKE SOME FOR YOURSELF AND YOUR SON. FOR THUS SAYS THE LORD GOD OF ISRAEL: 'THE BIN OF FLOUR SHALL

NOT BE USED UP, NOR SHALL THE JAR OF OIL RUN DRY, UNTIL THE DAY THE LORD SENDS RAIN ON THE EARTH.'"

I don't understand it. It's an amazing paradox to me. But what I see in the midst of the heavens seeming closed, in the midst of the drought, in the famine, in the midst of the heartache and the hardship and the challenge, is that God always finds a way to provide. It may be dry all around you. Maybe things didn't turn out how you thought they would. Maybe your prayers seemingly didn't get answered. But in that dry place, if you'll leave that brook, if you'll arise and go to where He has told you to go, there, in the midst of the heartache and the trouble, God will make provision for you. He will make a way. God has a way of filling the jar and the bin with amazing means in the middle of the heartache. That which is empty, only God can fill. Why did God send the prophet to a place that was going to dry up? Because God didn't want Elijah's

faith in a brook. The brook wasn't Elijah's source, God was.
God will lead you to places that seem dry to prove that place
is not your source, God is.

PART 02

A MOMENT ON MIRACLES

MIR·A·CLE /ˈMIRƏK(Ə)L/

The suspension of the laws of the ordinary course of nature.

A surprising and welcome event that is not explicable by natural or scientific laws and is therefore considered to be the work of a divine agency.

A highly improbable or extraordinary event, development, or accomplishment that brings very welcome consequences.

I want to talk to you now about miracles. More specifically, I want to talk about what to do when there is no miracle—when a miracle doesn't occur. But first, I want to be very clear as to what I believe from the beginning. What I believe, you may not necessarily believe. But I'm going to be clear about my beliefs and my position so you can better understand the angle from which I'm approaching this subject. I think there are many different worldviews that each of us could have, but if you look closely enough, you will see there are three views that I'll bring to your attention.

One worldview, or perspective of the world around us, could be the view that atheism holds. The atheistic view of life is simply that no God exists. That's the atheist's position. It's pretty evident that this is not the position I hold. Perhaps you hold that position. If so, I make no bones about it: I'm going to endeavor to persuade you away from that position.

The second worldview is the position of deism. Deism says there is a God who exists. He created the universe, but then He left the universe and His creation and chooses not to intervene any longer in that creation. So, there was once a God who set everything in motion, but He then left that creation to fend for itself. I don't hold to this position, either.

The third position is the position of theism. Theism simply believes there is one God, the Creator of the universe, who intervenes in the world and sustains a personal relationship with His creation. Probably many of us hold that position as a worldview. But to make matters even more complex, as if that isn't enough, within the world of theism, there are all kinds of divergent belief systems. There are doctrines that Baptists would hold, or Catholics would hold, or Episcopalians, or Lutherans, or Charismatics, or Pentecostals.

Within this idea of theism, there are many other types of

belief systems that an individual could hold. From the very beginning, I want you to understand this, because some things I say may leave you wondering what my belief is. My belief is that God created everything and that He does want to maintain a relationship with His creation. He does intervene in His creation through different acts, through His power and omnipotence. He intervenes and interacts with His creation. I want to say that from the very beginning. I also want to say that I believe God is a miracle-working God. However, I do not believe that the miraculous occurs with as much frequency as many people in the religious world would have you believe.

Now, I have a very challenging assignment in this book. My assignment is not to dissuade you from the miraculous potential that God has. I don't want you to abandon your belief in the miraculous, nor do I want you to be gullible and think that just because you want something of the miraculous to occur, it will occur. I did a bit of research and found that in the entire Scriptures, all four thousand years of humanity that is recorded in the Bible, there are just 120 miracles. Only 120 miracles are recorded within that four-thousand-year span of human history. If you do the math, that means that on average, there is just one miracle every thirty-three years or so. That means one person every thirty-three years would get a miracle. Why do I think this is important?

First Kings 17 is where I would like to look with you, starting in verse 1:

> **AND ELIJAH THE TISHBITE, OF THE INHABITANTS OF GILEAD, SAID TO AHAB, "AS THE LORD GOD OF ISRAEL LIVES, BEFORE WHOM I STAND, THERE SHALL NOT BE DEW NOR RAIN THESE YEARS, EXCEPT AT MY WORD." THEN THE WORD OF THE LORD CAME TO HIM, SAYING, "GET AWAY FROM HERE AND TURN EASTWARD, AND**

HIDE BY THE BROOK CHERITH, WHICH FLOWS INTO THE JORDAN. AND IT WILL BE THAT YOU SHALL DRINK FROM THE BROOK, AND I HAVE COMMANDED THE RAVENS TO FEED YOU THERE." SO HE WENT AND DID ACCORDING TO THE WORD OF THE LORD, FOR HE WENT AND STAYED BY THE BROOK CHERITH, WHICH FLOWS INTO THE JORDAN. THE RAVENS BROUGHT HIM BREAD AND MEAT IN THE MORNING, AND BREAD AND MEAT IN THE EVENING; AND HE DRANK FROM THE BROOK. AND IT HAPPENED AFTER A WHILE THAT THE BROOK DRIED UP, BECAUSE THERE HAD BEEN NO RAIN IN THE LAND.

I want to use this passage of Scripture as a metaphor to describe what I felt like, through the driest season in my life. To me, the phrase "the heavens seemed closed" is a great way to describe what had been going on in my world during this time. I'm not telling you this for you to feel bad about what went on in my world. I am telling you this with the hope and the expectation that you'll gain some understanding as I simply share my heart and what I've gone through. I may say some things that I'm not supposed to say, to be really transparent and honest with my thinking process and what I've gone through. That's all I have—my experience with what God's Word says. If you'll look at your life very closely, you'll see that's all you have, too, what your life experience has been up until this point. How you've sorted out God's plan for your life in good and bad situations, in good times and in challenging times, in easy seasons and in difficult seasons.

Elijah came to the point that God said there was not going to be any rain until He said differently. But God provided for him in the midst of that drought. Elijah was watered. Elijah had found sustenance at this brook, but then it dried up. I don't know exactly how Elijah felt about that, but *I* can say how I would feel. I would have questions like, "Okay, God, why was a drought necessary in the first place? Why not just let it keep on raining?" Have you ever wondered that? Why would God cause a drought? Or why not just make it easier and let all the plants grow, rather than giving the birds the assignment of delivering his supply? Why not just let it keep on raining? I don't understand it.

I'm not coming from the position that I have all the answers. The position that I have occupied is more that I have a lot of questions, and I'm okay with letting you know that. I have questions to which I don't have the answers. It just gets under my skin when believers have an I *know it all* mindset. To me, the mindset that says, "I know it all" is the beginning of ignorance. When someone says, "I know it all," what do you know about that person? You know that they don't know anything, because the wise person says, "The older I get, the more I realize I don't know." The longer I live, the more questions I have—not more answers. That's why I love the bumper sticker that says: *Hire a teenager while he or she still knows everything.* So many of us live as spiritual teenagers with a know-it-all attitude, but I definitely never want that for myself. Elijah didn't have that attitude. Paul describes this well in 1 Corinthians 13. In verse 11, he says this:

> **WHEN I WAS A CHILD, I SPOKE AS A CHILD, I UNDERSTOOD AS A CHILD, I THOUGHT AS A CHILD; BUT WHEN I BECAME A MAN, I PUT AWAY CHILDISH THINGS.**

How can you tell when a person is becoming an adult? It's not when they reach a certain age. It's when their habits and actions begin to change. It's not when they turn eighteen that they become an adult. It's not when they turn twenty-five or thirty that a person becomes an adult man or a woman. A person becomes a man or a woman whenever they say,

"These are childish things, and I'm no longer going to entertain them."

It's the same way with our thought life. Paul goes on in verses 12 and 13:

> **FOR NOW WE SEE IN A MIRROR, DIMLY, BUT THEN FACE TO FACE. NOW I KNOW IN PART, BUT THEN I SHALL KNOW JUST AS I ALSO AM KNOWN. AND NOW ABIDE FAITH, HOPE, LOVE, THESE THREE; BUT THE GREATEST OF THESE IS LOVE.**

Faith, hope, and love are what abide. I want to talk about hope, and specifically, I want to talk about the role of hope in our lives. When things don't go the way we wished they would have gone, what do we do?

As I've said many times, my mother was a woman of great faith. She passed away in March 2011 after fighting a good fight.

She ran a good race. Her death caused a lot of troubling in my heart about my beliefs and what I felt was true about God's Word, especially when it comes to the idea of miracles. I want to emphasize this very strongly. This is just *my experience*, and my personal struggle with this idea of the miraculous. I'm hopeful that you'll find in this story—in my story—something that will help you in your own life. I know that every word of my story will not fit perfectly into your current scenario. That would be an impossible task for someone to accomplish. I'm just hopeful that because I am open about some things, you'll see your own situation more clearly.

My mom's health battle lasted about four and a half years. After she was diagnosed, she shared the news with my wife and I. My mom was a beautician, and she had always styled my hair. She had come over to our house and was standing in our kitchen, cutting my hair. And just like that, in the middle of my haircut, she told me she'd been diagnosed with stage four melanoma. I didn't know what that meant. Not really. (Now I know there is no stage five.) But I did know what my default response was. I know what I had been conditioned to say and how I was supposed to respond in that kind of situation. My "spiritual" training had conditioned me so that anytime something challenging was announced, I would make a few confessions and a few decrees to magically cause that problem to disappear from my life. If you just make the right confession, I believed, then the problem will no longer be a problem. It will be erased from your life.

However, as life went on, my mother's condition worsened. As I prayed and sought God about the situation, I simply said, "Okay, God, what is going on? We don't seem to be getting the answers I think we ought to be getting. What is happening?" I struggle with sharing this, because I became aware that I've never expressed these thoughts. I can't tell you the timeline of when I became aware, but it was about halfway through the process that I began to have a knowing on the inside that I couldn't shake. It was the knowing that my mom wasn't going to make it. Inside of me, a war was being waged as I began to fear I was abandoning my faith.

To me, I felt like I was abandoning my belief in the supernatural. I was "being negative." I even questioned whether I had become displeasing to God. In the beginning of the process, thoughts would come that Mom wasn't going to make it through this. But I would begin to identify those thoughts, as many of us would, as the words of the enemy, and I would go through the ritual of saying, "No, I rebuke those thoughts in Jesus' name." I would feel guilty for entertaining those thoughts when everyone around me was saying, "There is a miracle just around the corner. Keep hope alive that this situation is going to turn around and change."

That's a very challenging thing to hear when on the inside, you know what the outcome is going to be, but you aren't ready to accept yet what you know is true.

This applies in all kinds of different areas of our lives. It applies in relationships—when we know that a relationship is ending but we live in a state of denial, not wanting to accept that what we're sensing in our heart is true. I was reminded of these words of Jesus:

> **"I STILL HAVE MANY THINGS TO SAY TO YOU, BUT YOU CANNOT BEAR THEM NOW. HOWEVER, WHEN HE, THE SPIRIT OF TRUTH, HAS COME, HE WILL GUIDE YOU INTO ALL TRUTH; FOR HE WILL NOT SPEAK ON HIS OWN AUTHORITY, BUT WHATEVER HE HEARS HE WILL SPEAK; AND HE WILL TELL YOU THINGS TO COME."**
>
> **—JOHN 16:12-13**

Now, there are only two options with regard to these words of Jesus. Either that passage of Scripture is true or it's not true. Either God, by His Spirit, will show us the things to come or He won't. I believe that He will. I believe that God does show us things to come, but at the time of my mother's illness, a war was raging inside of me, against the false belief that everything He shows us that is to come must be positive. Falsely, I thought that He would only show me good things that were going to take place. That's a very convenient belief to hold. It makes you feel better. It can make you more comfortable with the situation, but it is not necessarily the truth. And the truth is what I'm after. The truth, I believe, is what we ought to love more than anything else on this planet. Someone might ask, "Well, what about Jesus? Shouldn't we love Him more?"

It is impossible to love Jesus more than the truth. "Why?,"

you might ask. Because Jesus *is* the truth. We are to love the truth, which is Him. Jesus said, "I am the way, I am the truth, and I am the life." When you love the truth, you love Jesus. God, by His Spirit, was trying to show me something that was to come. He was trying to prepare me. But because what I was sensing in my spirit didn't fit with what I wanted to embrace— because I was like Elijah at the brook that was drying up, and I didn't want it to dry up—I began to "reject" the thought that my mother was not going to beat the cancer. I fought hard against that thought. But when God shows you something to come, whether it's good or whether it's bad in its outcome, He is showing it to you for your good and for your benefit. But here's what happens. Many people abandon their hope, or many have hope that is misplaced because they're fighting to believe something that is contrary to the truth. They're fighting against what God is endeavoring to reveal to them.

Why do we deny those things? There is a whole host of reasons that caused me to live in denial at that time. Believing that you have some sort of control over a situation that is outside of your control is definitely one motivation. The human psyche loves to say, "I'm in control of this situation. I really am in control. All I have to do is make these confessions and speak healing over my body."

I struggled with this for months. I struggled with the idea that I was letting my mom down, that I was letting my dad down, that I was letting my sister and my wife and kids down. I thought if I could just switch my heart to believe that the miracle would come, then it would come. Somehow I felt I was the linchpin, the reason God wasn't moving in this situation—because I was the one entertaining thoughts of doubt and unbelief.

I beat myself up over my "negative" thoughts night and day.

I continued to beat myself up over this even after my mom passed away. I wondered whether the outcome would have been different if I could have switched to positive thoughts in my spirit. Have you ever struggled with that? I hope the brief words I'm about to share will help you through that situation.

In January 2011, my mom was in the room upstairs where she put on her makeup. She called me up there, asking me to come up there alone. I don't know if you've ever had this experience, but there are certain times when you're invited into a conversation and something begins to happen inside you. It is as though a million butterflies are loose inside your chest cavity. There's not necessarily any pain, but there's all kinds of emotion going on. I knew this conversation was important.

When I arrived in her room, Mom said, "Josh, I want to talk to you about some things. And I want them to be only between you and me until the time comes for you to share them with others."

"How will I know the time to share these things with others?" I asked.

Mom responded simply, "You'll know."

And I do know. Now is the time to share what Mom told me.

Mom told me she knew that she was at the end of her life. She told me she knew there was no miracle coming. And she told me she was okay with that. She wasn't afraid. She was willing to embrace, in her words, "whatever is next for me." That was the first time another human being said to me what I already knew inside my heart.

When Mom began to say these things, I didn't say anything in response. I didn't need to say anything, but a level of comfort and help engulfed me. Proverbs 13:12 says this:

> **HOPE DEFERRED MAKES THE HEART SICK,**
>
> **BUT WHEN THE DESIRE COMES, IT IS A TREE OF LIFE.**

She asked me a question that stunned me. "Am I a disappointment to you?" "What?!" I exclaimed. "Why would you ask me that? No, of course not."

"Are you disappointed that I didn't stay married to your dad? Are you disappointed in me as a mom? Are you disappointed that I didn't have enough faith to be healed?"

It was in that moment that I chose to change the way I spoke to people. I came to the realization that people thought they were responsible for the rain. We are not. We seek the Kingdom. We do our part. God always does His part.

Many times, we place our hope in a situation or a circumstance that we shouldn't. We hope for something we ought not hope for. And the result is discouragement, disappointment, and disillusion when what we hope for does not come to pass. The heavens seem closed when we project our own fears onto a situation and then choose to believe that everything is within our control. No man controls God. No man controls the outcome of certain situations. You cannot, by an act of your will, cause the miraculous to take place. If you and I could do that, miracles would constantly be happening all over the planet.

Still, don't forget that I *do* believe in the miraculous. And I don't plan on ever abandoning my belief in the miraculous. But what we need is a *balanced* approach to the miraculous. What we need to understand is that regardless of our own personal experience, bias, or belief system, nothing in the Scriptures indicates a human being can simply will a miracle to take place. There are no examples of someone desiring something badly enough, for some to just want it enough, that they could make it happen. To the contrary. Paul made it very clear in his writings that miraculous events, the suspension of the laws of the ordinary course of nature, *only* happen as God wills them, not as we do.

You might be wondering why I would try to take away your "hope for the miraculous." The truth is, I'm not taking away your hope; I'm *giving* you hope in your heart—just in a way you might not understand. Hope is destroyed when it is misplaced, when you just keep your fingers crossed and "hope for the best" in a situation. When you realize that the outcome you hope for will not likely occur, this isn't an act of doubt or unbelief.

It is a risk for me to say these things, because some people might think I just don't believe in miracles because of my grief following my mother's death. That isn't true. I do believe in the miraculous, but the "miracles" we see in life are not as frequent as some people would like us to believe. In fact, the miraculous does not occur nearly as frequently as I wish it did. I wish miracles were far more frequent than they are, but by their very nature, by their very definition, they cannot be.

When individuals seem to think that miracles happen just because they want them to, it bothers me because it can sow discontent and seeds of harm in people's lives. When the miracle doesn't come—and most likely it will not—their faith and hope can be rocked, even harmed, because they had all of their hope and all of their faith put into this one failsafe miracle, this one get-out-of-jail-free card. And when it doesn't occur, it warps, distorts, and cheapens the cross of Calvary and the saving act of Christ. Saying that you can just have a miracle whenever you want it, because you want it, cheapens the nature of God and leads people into despair and disappointment. When the miracle doesn't take place, then individuals will ask, "What's wrong with me? If only I had prayed more… If only I had done more… If only I had given more… If only I had… If only I had… If only I had…"

When the situation calls for the miraculous and then no miracle comes, I submit to you that, then and there, the believer has the opportunity to occupy a new position. They can declare, "No matter what happens in this life, I do not have to surrender hope. I do not have to surrender hope, because the One who loved me, who died for me, has given me a hope and a future."

Our hope does not lie only in this life. It doesn't lie in what happens to us here on this planet. And the here and now is not where our hope is to be placed. Our hope is to be firmly planted in what Christ has already done for us, whether the miracle comes or not, whether the situation changes or not.

We've been examining the life of Elijah in 1 Kings 17. We can see Elijah is given this message from God that there's going to be a drought in the land. He shares this message with the king in the region, and God makes a way for him and provides for his needs. The Lord sends him to a brook, but the brook where God sent him soon dries up. We can use this as a kind of metaphor, as an idea, an illustration, and a picture of how we examine our lives.

When it seems as if the heavens are closed, that God isn't really hearing us, or maybe we feel like God has somehow abandoned us, we need a new perspective. I've been sharing some very personal things with you in this book. My mom passed away in 2011 after battling melanoma for over four years, and I've endeavored to very candidly share in a heartfelt way my response to that situation. My background gave me the impression that if something bad were to happen in my life, or if one of my loved ones became ill, I simply needed to do a few certain things and the problem would be remedied and made right by the Lord. And, conversely, if it wasn't made right, then something must have been wrong with *me*. If your loved one didn't get healed…if you went through a divorce…if you experienced any kind of major challenge in your life…then you just didn't have enough faith to get through the situation successfully. I don't know if you've ever heard anything like that or had these thoughts yourself.

For many people, the holidays are amazing. Having family and friends near is always wonderful, but many other people have a tough time during the holiday season. They remember the way life "used to be," loved ones who aren't there anymore, relationships and families that are broken. It can be very challenging at this time of year, when everyone around us seems to be having a wonderful time. In the same way, when we hear how God does such awesome miracles for other people, it's amazing, but there are people who wonder why those things don't seem to be happening to them. Where are the people of God left when church leaders don't talk about the not-so-popular topics from time to time? People need to know what to do when the answer doesn't come in time, when the challenge doesn't end with a happily-ever-after. I'm concerned that we pick and choose the things we focus on, and it seems more popular among church leaders, in order to fill more seats, to talk about the more spectacular and amazing things that God may be doing.

You shouldn't only be interested in the things of God that make you feel good, although most people gravitate toward that, looking for a feel-good experience. Don't get me wrong—I am all for positive thoughts and experiences. I don't want you to be miserable and not enjoy your life. I *want* you to enjoy life. Your spouse wants you to enjoy life. The point I'm making is that we tend to gravitate toward the things that make us feel good when really the aim of the believer should be to learn the truth. The *truth* is what Jesus said would make us free. What makes us feel good may not set us free. It may not liberate our hearts. It may not liberate our minds. It may not give you a proper worldview. It may not give you a Christ-centered perspective. If we're after a *God-centered* view of the world around us, then we must look at *all* parts of Scripture, including the verses we're not so excited about at first. That's why we are looking at Elijah and the challenging time he and his nation went through.

This verse out of James sums up the story, I think, quite well James wrote that Elijah was a man with passions. He was just like us. That's important.

A MOMENT ON MIRACLES **073**

> **ELIJAH WAS A MAN WITH A NATURE LIKE OURS, AND HE PRAYED EARNESTLY THAT IT WOULD NOT RAIN; AND IT DID NOT RAIN ON THE LAND FOR THREE YEARS AND SIX MONTHS. AND HE PRAYED AGAIN, AND THE HEAVEN GAVE RAIN, AND THE EARTH PRODUCED ITS FRUIT.**
>
> **—JAMES 5:17–18**

Now let's look at 1 Kings 18 and check out the end of this story. But before we do, I want you to remember that truth: Elijah was a man, just like us. Think about that for a minute. Elijah was subject to the same emotions, pain, disappointment, challenges, joys, and sorrows that we have experienced. He was just the same as us. Yes, God used him in a special way to minister to the people of Israel. He was assigned to be a prophet. So, he had an amazing assignment, but he still was a human being—just like us. He had hurts and pains. He had to deal with certain things.

First Kings 18:41–47 tells the end of the story. After the drought was over, after three and a half years, Elijah had a showdown with the prophets of Baal, and he called fire down from heaven and burned up the enemies of God. The people then repented and returned to God.

> THEN ELIJAH SAID TO AHAB, "GO UP, EAT AND DRINK; FOR THERE IS THE SOUND OF ABUNDANCE OF RAIN." SO AHAB WENT UP TO EAT AND DRINK. AND ELIJAH WENT UP TO THE TOP OF CARMEL; THEN HE BOWED DOWN ON THE GROUND, AND PUT HIS FACE BETWEEN HIS KNEES, AND SAID TO HIS SERVANT, "GO UP NOW, LOOK TOWARD THE SEA." SO HE WENT UP AND LOOKED, AND SAID, "THERE IS NOTHING." AND SEVEN TIMES HE SAID, "GO AGAIN." THEN IT CAME TO PASS THE SEVENTH TIME, THAT HE SAID, "THERE IS A CLOUD, AS SMALL AS A MAN'S HAND, RISING OUT OF THE SEA!" SO HE SAID, "GO UP, SAY TO AHAB, 'PREPARE YOUR CHARIOT, AND GO DOWN

BEFORE THE RAIN STOPS YOU.'" NOW IT HAPPENED IN THE MEANTIME THAT THE SKY BECAME BLACK WITH CLOUDS AND WIND, AND THERE WAS A HEAVY RAIN.

So, let's get this picture in our minds. James tells us that Elijah is a man just like us who prayed earnestly. In 1 Kings 18, Elijah prayed earnestly seven times. James tells us that Elijah made an earnest prayer. And in 1 Kings we see what this earnest prayer looked like. Now, maybe you have a different picture of what earnest prayer might mean, but stay with me. The Scripture says that Elijah bowed to the ground and put his head between his knees. As he was praying, in my mind, he probably was banging the ground. He was probably sweating. In my mind, he's not smiling. He's sincere. He's very determined. He's like, "Dear God, You said the rain would come. It's been three and a half years. Please. I'm begging You." Then Elijah rose, got all the way up, and then did it all over again. He did this *seven times*.

Elijah made an earnest prayer. I can identify with this, and I wonder if you do too. But just like we've talked about, faith is not about receiving a get-out-of-jail-free card. It's not about avoiding the challenges. Faith determines how you walk *through* that fire. Faith determines your attitude; it influences how you talk and how you live and how your attitude will be with God when things aren't going your way. Anybody can worship God when the sun is shining and you're getting everything your heart desires. Anybody can do that.

I'll share a personal story, not to pull on your emotions, but to show you that this is real life. When Mom was going through her health challenges, the crises of life came our way. One night in particular we were at the emergency room, and the service was incredibly slow. Whatever is the opposite of a "complainer," my mom was that person. But this evening, she was in a lot of pain. She couldn't get comfortable being seated, and she couldn't get comfortable standing up. Tumors in different parts of her body were infringing on nerves and tendons and other things that caused her to be absolutely riddled with pain. Mom was not one to show much that she was in pain, but on this day, she was trying to get comfortable, and she grabbed hold of me. She buried her head in my chest, grabbed hold of me with both hands, and began to magnify God out loud with her voice. I was like, *Whoa!* I probably would have been cussing. I know you think I'm more sanctified than that, but when I am in that much pain, a voice rises in me that I'm not comfortable with. I saw the pressure and the pain my mom was experiencing. I could see it in her face. When she grabbed hold of me, she squeezed my arms as she magnified the Lord. I was amazed, and I realized I wanted to do the same. Attitudes are contagious. Whatever attitude you bring to your situation, others will follow your lead.

I knew that worshiping God was the right thing to do. But I have to say, I identified with the description of Elijah we have been considering. At that time, I had been pushing every button, pulling every lever, reciting every prayer I ever knew to say. I was rebuking this and commanding that. I was speaking life and doing everything else I knew to do.

Still, the sky was cloudless. The heavens seemed closed to me. So I began to do other things. I'm a guy with normal emotions. That night, as my mom was magnifying the Lord, I magnified the Lord with her—a little bit, but not nearly as long as she did. I finally decided I needed to do something about her pain, so I went over to the desk, found a nurse, and said, "I need you to get on this situation right now."

"Sir," she said, "we're waiting for this..." She went on to tell me a host of problems they were dealing with.

So, I went back to my family, and Mom was still magnifying the Lord. I am just trying to describe the situation to you, but I was in a state of mind that was ready to do anything. I was desperate to change the situation.

As a side note, desperation is an amazing force that can be used by God or be used by the enemy. We can get so desperate in our situations on this earth that we decide, "I don't care what God's Word says. I'm just going to do what I want to do, because I need this to change so that we can get some results." That is how Ishmael was conceived in the Old Testament—by Abraham deciding to do his own thing. We don't really want an 'Ishmael,' though; what we're after is our 'Isaac'—that is, God's plan and God's will for our lives.

I'm not proud of this, but I left the room again, and I found that same nurse. I said, "Listen, apparently, I wasn't as clear as I should have been when I spoke to your earlier. So here's what's going to happen. Either a doctor comes in here and does something to manage my mother's pain, or the police are going to be taking me out of here in handcuffs."

The nurse didn't really like my words and my tone too much, but it wasn't much longer before they called my mother back and a doctor began to treat her pain. What's the point of this story? Well, I was in a state of desperation—the same state I imagine Elijah was in, where I think we all have been before, where we desperately want something to change, but the heavens seem closed. The earth seems dry. The answer seems far away. However, Elijah gives us a good example to follow: He was persistent; seven times he refused to quit.

Some of us pray for fifteen minutes and expect the answer to be hand-delivered to us by UPS. We pray a few times, then go to the door and start looking in the mailbox, or we look at our social media feeds. We look at our email to see if someone has sent us the answer. If we pray a second time and we still don't get results, most of us give up and say, "Well, I'm done with that." Most of us would never think to try *seven times.*

To me, Elijah's story speaks of persistence. It may speak different things to you, but to me, I can see that Elijah would not quit. He would not stop. And just like you and me, Elijah had different thoughts while he was praying. While he was seeking God for the answers, thoughts crept in. And in Elijah's case, his life was literally on the line, because if he told the people he was speaking for God and he was not, he would have been killed. His neck was on the line, and he still wouldn't quit. He wouldn't stop.

Thoughts came to Elijah: *Man, it isn't going to work for you. God has abandoned you. God isn't gonna answer this one.*

You've obviously done something to cause God's favor to no longer shine upon you. All those thoughts that you and I deal with, he dealt with them, too. He was a real guy, a real person who dealt with those very real thoughts.

Persistence means "to fight through" something. How many of us, when the heavens seemed closed, when no answer seems to be coming, have ever had the thought as our first response: *I must have done something to make God angry?*

I'm not suggesting you just go out and do any old thing you want to do. I'm not advocating that you go out and knowingly do wrong, but I do want you to live with this consciousness: that God is incredibly in love with each and every one of us. He loved us so much that He sent His Son to die so that we could live eternally with Him. The Bible tells us that there is nothing that can separate us from the love of God. The amazing reality of God's love for us is what many of us need to really embrace. We need not just to hear the words spoken to us over and over, but we need to embrace the knowledge that God truly cares for us, loves us, and is looking out for us. What's going on in the world around us is not a determining factor, is not a telltale sign, of whether or not God loves us.

We need to settle this once and for all. God loves us with a great and everlasting love. Don't think Elijah didn't have to fight through the idea that God might be angry with him. When the idea that God is angry with us is reinforced by people who are viewed as godly leaders, it tends to bring condemnation and fear and difficulty in people's lives. When God says, "There is now no condemnation to those who are in Christ Jesus," does that mean we are perfect? No, far from it.

If perfection is required after we begin to follow Christ, we are all without hope!

Perfection is not the requirement; what is required is humility, receiving grace and mercy, and truth, receiving the power to change, and doing things differently. The opportunity to look at life through the lens of God's Word is what it's all about. That is what we should be after as Christ-followers, not to be content making errors. Instead, we must admit that we make mistakes and then learn from them, grow from them, and move to another place, bringing others along with us.

I will be honest with you. When my mom passed away, I struggled with these types of thoughts: *What did I do to deserve this? Did I do something wrong? Could I have done something differently? Could I have changed the outcome? God, I don't understand. I just don't understand.*

The good news is that there is not a question you can ask of the Lord that will cause Him to be offended. If it's a cry from your heart, if it's what your heart seeks an answer for, ask. He says "ask and you'll receive; seek and you'll find; knock and it will be opened to you." So many people live in a captive mindset that says, 'I'm not allowed to ask that question. I'm supposed to just be a good soldier of the Lord and recognize that I can't understand everything. God doesn't owe me an answer.' All of that is true. God may not owe you an answer, but if you have a question, it is still okay to ask.

I was speaking with a lady after church one week. She caught me after I left to greet the congregation. She had tears in her eyes because she was going through the very same struggles, the same thoughts, that I had when my mother died. One of her family members was ill, and she had been asking the questions: *Did I do something wrong? Was there something I could have done differently?* Sickness and disease, heartaches and challenges—we don't have to like them, but they are a part of life on this planet. Life is riddled with limitations and challenges and difficulties. I could find some Scripture references that might convince you that you can avoid all problems in your life, but I would be doing you a disservice. I wouldn't be doing my job.

What I *can* tell you is this: When we go through challenges, if we have Christ as the center and the source of our lives, no matter what the outcome is, we win. No matter what happens at the end of what you are experiencing, you win. How can I say that? Because Paul said that God always causes us to triumph. He always causes us to win. It may not look like I'm winning. It may look like I'm losing. But don't worry what it looks like. Don't worry what's right in front of you, because God will come through. He'll send the rain. You can be like Elijah if you choose to get up. When Elijah gets up, it speaks to me of an attitude he had. His attitude was this: *I'm going to look at the very smallest, seemingly insignificant thing. I'm going to look for something on the horizon. I'm going to look for anything I can be thankful for, on which I can build my faith, and I will grow and be full of hope and courage and strength.*

Then Elijah saw a cloud that was the size of a man's hand. All that the people around him saw was a seemingly insignificant cloud. But the Bible says Elijah heard the sound of the abundance of rain when he saw that cloud. Even when the heavens seem closed, I hope you'll realize it only *seems* that way. Because Christ died for us, we forever live under an *open heaven.* We live under a heaven that allows us to communicate with God, to offer our thoughts and our prayers, our deepest emotions, our heartfelt feelings to Him. If we all lived this one verse—just this one verse—for the rest of our lives, it would be amazing. Life would be amazing, notwithstanding the difficulty. Look at what Paul says in Philippians 4:6:

BE ANXIOUS FOR NOTHING.

The Amplified Version says it this way: "Do not be anxious or worried about anything."

> **BE ANXIOUS FOR NOTHING, BUT IN EVERYTHING BY PRAYER AND SUPPLICATION, WITH THANKSGIVING, LET YOUR REQUESTS BE MADE KNOWN TO GOD.**

Paul says that when we offer these prayers with an attitude of thanksgiving, when we see and are thankful for the small things in our lives, the small clouds on the horizon, when we give thanks and let our requests be made known to Him and share our hearts with Him, that's when He says, "And the peace of God, which surpasses all understanding will guard your hearts and minds through Christ Jesus." How amazing it is that the peace of God can come in the middle of the storms, in the middle of the heartache, in the middle of the difficulties. God's looking out to guard your heart and your mind through Jesus Christ.

If I can sum up everything I would like to say, it would be this: When difficult things happen, don't question whether God loves you. He does love you—always and forever. The question is, when difficult things happen, will you love Him back?

I'll tell you what my choice is going to be: my choice is still to look up at the seemingly cloudless sky until I see a cloud the size of a man's hand, and then I will say, "I hear the sound of God's abundance of rain over my life." My choice is to take God at His Word even through the fire and the rain and the storm and the problematic situations. Having to look at my children as they weep and mourn the loss of their beloved grandmother, going through those challenging things, seeing their faces, and knowing what they felt, I still choose to believe. You have a choice, and it's yours to make. It may not be easy, but it will be worth it.

Like the prophet says, "as for me and my house, we will serve the Lord" (see Joshua 24:15). In both the good stuff and the bad stuff, we will serve the Lord. Why? Because He reigns and rules. He is the King of kings and the Lord of lords. He is not to be begged or bargained with. He is not to be negotiated with. He is the Supreme Ruler over our lives and over the entire earth. He is the Creator of all things. He is the Giver of life. He is the Alpha and the Omega, the beginning and the end. He's the first and the last. He is everything that you can imagine Him to be and then He's more. He's all you will ever need and then some. He is more than enough. If you do not know Him, if you are going through this life without Him, I want you to have the chance to change your mind and begin to follow the One who laid down His life so that you might live.

I wish I could look you square in the eyes to say this: God loved you so much that He gave His only Son to die for you so that you could live. And if you're going through this life without Him, you should make a change. God sets before us life and death, blessings and curses. And in case we're not sharp enough to get the right answer to that choice we should make, He tells us, "Therefore, choose life!"

While Jesus was here on the earth, He said, "I am the way, the truth and the life, no man can come to the Father except through Me." He also said, "If you confess Me before men, I'll confess you before My Father, but if you deny Me before men, I'll deny you before My Father." He did not give us room for anything other than to make the choice. Either He is a lunatic, He is a liar, or He is the Lord and God of all. There is no other choice in the matter.

In Acts 13, Paul wrote of David's God-ordained purpose, used to serve his own generation, the reason he had when he occupied the earth:

> **NOW WHEN DAVID HAD SERVED GOD'S PURPOSE IN HIS OWN GENERATION, HE FELL ASLEEP; HE WAS BURIED WITH HIS ANCESTORS AND HIS BODY DECAYED.**
>
> **—ACTS 13:36 NIV**

In other words, David finished the assignment and the purpose that God placed on his life, and then he went over into the next life. What I hope for each of us is that we have a growing passion to find God's purpose for our lives on a deeper level. Each of us has a divine purpose to serve the world in which we live. These words are for you, and they are for me. I say that because often in the Church, what I'm doing as a pastor is viewed as a God-given purpose, but what everyone else does is just busywork. We need to dispel that idea and break that mindset, because each of us has been given a divine purpose to serve our generation, and no two purposes look identical. The reason our purposes don't look the same is one of the reasons I want to have this conversation with you, because the thing that makes your purpose and my purpose different from everyone else's on the planet is your life's story. Your life's context and the impact you have on the world around you is a story that nobody else has, right? You're on a journey that no one else has traveled before. You have DNA that is not shared in its totality with anyone else on the planet. Everything I say to you, you can look up on Google and you can find similar statements. But what you cannot download, what you cannot find on Google, is my life story and the emotions I have attached to my experience. You can't download that from anywhere. It's wonderful that I'm not downloadable—but neither are you. This conversation is a part of my life's purpose, to do something that I think is unpleasant, which is talk about things that nobody else seems to be talking about.

Here's what you need to know. I feel very insecure about this entire idea that we're going to discuss. Doesn't that make you feel safe? Let me just pull the curtain back and show you into my life for a moment, not to highlight me, but to show that it's okay to be a human being. I never know if I'm learning enough to serve you properly. I never know if I know enough to help you where you are in life. I never know if I have the right words or the right language to share. I'm often insecure that somebody else has a better way of communicating with a better ability to grab and keep your attention. I'm positive there are people on the planet whose story is far more captivating than mine. I'm positive there are many people on the planet who have gone through much worse situations than I have. All of this was going on inside my head, as my thoughts admonished me: *Josh, you really don't have what it takes, and this really isn't going to be helpful. You're really just wasting people's time.* I don't know if you've felt that about your life, but I sometimes feel that way about my life. I want to completely disarm this idea we all have by giving voice to something I've never really heard anyone openly share and discuss before.

Really, if I'm going to say it the way I see it, the Church is giving permission for you to hide the real you from everybody else. Church has become a place to hide behind a fake mask and say, "No, let's just act like this." Just smile and act like everything's okay, when what's going on inside of your world is ripping you apart. Emotionally, you are being dragged through difficult challenges and circumstances, and you come in the Church and you see everybody else smile, and they've got joy and they've got laughter and they're talking to other people. And on the inside, you're angry. You're discontented, you're discouraged, and you're depressed, but you're not allowed to say it for fear of being judged, criticized, and given a hard time for not being at the top of your game.

What I say to all that is, "Phooey!" We're going to break that model and start a new one.

I'll go first. I'm just going to lead the way and do my best to muddle through, and hope that my words somehow find you in the place where you are, so that you can take steps forward. This journey began in 2011 after my mom had finished a forty-four-month-long battle with cancer. Everyone in our family was praying, believing, standing, and expecting her to receive a miracle. The idea was this: "Man, if God's ever done a miracle for anybody, certainly He'll do it for Angie. She's an amazing lady. She's such a godly woman. She loves prayer. She loves her kids. Certainly God will do a miracle in her life."

All our hearts were expecting that physical healing, that miracle to occur, but it didn't. So, what I want to discuss with you is something that's very unpleasant, but it's something each of us has to face from time to time. The issue is, how do we navigate life? When the miracle does happen, it's easy to navigate life. When the miracle does happen, you shout, you dance, you smile, you do something great. You express how you feel; you fill out a card and tell somebody how great God is. But when the miracle doesn't happen, that's when everybody leaves you alone. That's when nobody knows what to say. When the answer that was supposed to come doesn't come, everybody's confused and frustrated. It's when the marriage didn't work, after we thought God was going to give us a supernatural turnaround, that we have questions, and we get angry, and we pursue things that aren't in our best interest. It's when the finances don't get a supernatural turnaround that we have to face the reality of failure. We realize, *This isn't working the way I thought it was going to work. I've pushed every button, and I've pulled every lever.*

I've prayed every prayer I know to pray, and I've read every verse that I know to read, but it seems like heaven keeps saying no. That's when we need the people of God and the power of God in our lives like never before. That's when we need encouragement!

The story of Elijah in 1 Kings is why I titled this book *When the Heavens Seem Closed.* A deeper dive into this metaphor was helpful to me in my grieving process, and it gave me the language I needed to assign to what I didn't have language for.

I hope it helps you to assign an idea to something that maybe has just been kind of scattered and floating around in your mind, those things that you really haven't been able to get your hands on yet.

First Kings 17:1 speaks of Elijah:

AND ELIJAH THE TISHBITE, OF THE INHABITANTS OF GILEAD, SAID TO AHAB, "AS THE LORD GOD OF ISRAEL LIVES, BEFORE WHOM I STAND, THERE SHALL NOT BE DEW NOR RAIN THESE YEARS, EXCEPT AT MY WORD."

Ahab was the king of the land, and he and Elijah didn't really get along. He didn't treat Elijah very well over the course of his reign. It's somewhat understated in this passage of Scripture, but Ahab was a really wicked guy. And so it took courage and boldness for Elijah to say what he said to this wicked king. This was courageous because this was a time and a place when they would often kill the messenger. You've heard the phrase, "Don't kill the messenger"? That came from long ago, when people would give messages that those in authority didn't like. The messenger would be given a death sentence as a consequence for bringing the message that they had carried.

Elijah brought a message to Ahab from the Lord that simply

said this: "The rain is going to stop, King Ahab." His life was about to dry up. Challenges were about to invade his world.

When I read this passage of Scripture in the days and weeks after my mom's passing, this phrase jumped off the page at me. The language I attached to it was "when the heavens seem closed," because concerning everything I was looking at, it felt like I was living under a dried-up time with no more rain, no more help, no more encouragement. It was an incredibly difficult season. This is how I began to describe the journey that maybe you've experienced or are still experiencing. It's the journey of the barren soul, the dry and thirsty soul, the place where our emotions come, our decisions come, our thinking comes, and it's all dried up.

> **THEN THE WORD OF THE LORD CAME TO HIM, SAYING, "GET AWAY FROM HERE AND TURN EASTWARD, AND HIDE BY THE BROOK CHERITH, WHICH FLOWS INTO THE JORDAN. AND IT WILL BE THAT YOU SHALL**

DRINK FROM THE BROOK, AND I HAVE COMMANDED THE RAVENS TO FEED YOU THERE." SO HE WENT AND DID ACCORDING TO THE WORD OF THE LORD, FOR HE WENT AND STAYED BY THE BROOK CHERITH, WHICH FLOWS INTO THE JORDAN. THE RAVENS BROUGHT HIM BREAD AND MEAT IN THE MORNING, AND BREAD AND MEAT IN THE EVENING; AND HE DRANK FROM THE BROOK.

—1 KINGS 17:2–6

Elijah was given a respite from the drought, a break from the famine. He got a bit of water at a dry and thirsty point in his life. God provided for him.

AND IT HAPPENED AFTER A WHILE THAT THE BROOK DRIED UP, BECAUSE THERE HAD BEEN NO RAIN IN THE LAND.

—VERSE 7

Let me start by saying this: For each person reading this,

there's a truth you must acknowledge sooner or later: You're going to have a "dried-up-brook" moment sooner or later in life. If you haven't experienced it already, maybe you're experiencing it now. There's going to come a time when you come to a place where God used to provide in a certain way, but now that provision is all dried up. It's a change of season. Something is different. It's not like it used to be. And you're going to go through the pain of that transition. As you try to figure out a new normal in life, you will need to navigate through the thing that you've never had to navigate through before. And that's why this is so important—because what do you do when you don't know what to do? What is your heart going to do? Do you stay stuck? Do you get angry? What do you do?

I had so many questions for God. And I had to learn that was okay. I grew up in an environment in which people were not allowed to ask God anything. If that statement wasn't directly made, it was certainly implied. The idea was, "Who are you? He's *God*, so don't even ask Him about it. Don't ask. Don't question." But suddenly, I had all kinds of questions for God. Can I tell you something? When you ask God a question, He is strong enough to handle it—even the most difficult question you could ask. In other words, He isn't intimidated, rattled, or even annoyed by your questions. This is important because so many times, we have questions, but they go unspoken. And then resentment builds up in your soul, not toward a person, but toward God. Anger begins to fester, and the brook dries up.

You can become mad because you don't understand what to do now that the brook has dried up. You don't know where to go. You don't know what steps to take. Amos 8 describes it perfectly:

> **"BEHOLD, THE DAYS ARE COMING," SAYS THE LORD GOD, "THAT I WILL SEND A FAMINE ON THE LAND, NOT A FAMINE OF BREAD, NOR A THIRST FOR WATER, BUT OF HEARING THE WORDS OF THE LORD."**
>
> **—AMOS 8:11**

God gives you a warning. He says, "Here's a heads-up—something's coming your way. Something's headed down the path!" He was about to send a famine on the land—not a famine of bread, nor a thirst for water, but of hearing the words of the Lord.

Don't quit reading. Go to Part 03.

PART 03

SURVIVING THE FAMINE

CAUSES OF FAMINE

1. extreme drought

2. war

3. pestilence (locusts, or something that gets in and has an adverse effect on the agricultural system).

My mom's death acted as a trigger for me for a dried-up-brook moment, and that resulted in an emotional and spiritual famine in my life. Famine occurs for three reasons in the Scriptures, it is due either to:

1. EXTREME DROUGHT

2. WAR

3. PESTILENCE (LOCUSTS, OR SOMETHING THAT GETS IN AND HAS AN ADVERSE EFFECT ON THE AGRICULTURAL SYSTEM).

The language I'm using is this one of drought, of dryness that comes our way. Theologically, when damage and destructive things happen, what you need to understand is God is the builder. He's not the destroyer. There is an enemy to our souls who is working in this world. His name is Satan, and his desire for our lives is to steal from us, to kill us, and to destroy us.

We have to get this straight. God is not the enemy! Jesus' job description is to give us life and to give it to us more abundantly. God is not a destroyer; the enemy is. Jesus is the healer, the restorer, and the repairer of broken things—which often is us! You also need to understand this. I'm not trying to examine in detail why my mom passed away from cancer, because here's the truth: I don't get it. I don't know. I don't know why that happened.

An individual years ago came into my office and offered a suggestion as to why my mom died, and here's what they said to me. (I'm going to say this because I hope it offends you enough that you never say this yourself to a hurting person.) This individual came to me and said, "Josh, I can't help but think your mom was not healed because you tolerate divorce in this church."

Let that sink in for a second. Someone literally attributed the death of my mother to other people's failed relationships, people whom I had no control over. This person believed the actions of other people—and subsequently the death of my mother—to be my fault. Can I just say something here? We need to get rid of superstition, unlearned thinking, and false beliefs in the Church. Can we just stop being dumb? My response, which you might be curious about, was this: "I'm not sure if you've noticed, but people are getting divorced all over the world. Without my permission." God does not hold me responsible for something that is someone else's responsibility. I can be responsible *to* you, but I can't be responsible *for* you.

I want you to understand that I have not once ever gone down a complete path to find out why my mom lost her life to cancer. Knowing why wouldn't necessarily solve my emotional dilemma, my emotional famine, and it won't fix yours, either.

Don't let curiosity get the better of you and stand between you and moving forward in your relationship with God. Don't let what you don't know stop you from doing what you do know to do. Because as the day is long, you will always have questions, and so will I—and that's okay. You've got to know that. As these things settled into my soul, I felt the famine grow inside my heart. Maybe you have felt this way, too. I felt unmotivated. I felt unworthy. I felt unloved at times. I even felt unsaved. I felt lost. Keep in mind, in 2011, I was doing my best to pastor a church. And what I'm telling you might be shocking. It might bother you. You might even judge me. You might have criticism for me in how I handled the situation and what I did. And you know what? I'm finally at a place where I'm okay with you not being okay with how I responded. My heart is to help others go through it differently than the way I did. I'm tired of preachers not being authentic, not telling you what's actually going on in their world. I will not be that way. I refuse to be that way. I refuse to allow my desire for you to think well of me prevent me from saying the things that went on inside of me. I believe that if I let it out and tell it all, it will help you. And I'd rather look like a fool and be embarrassed than not help you through your own situation. Yes, some of the things I'm telling you are embarrassing to me. I'm going to tell you straight-up, I did it wrong. I didn't handle the situation properly, but I did the best I knew how to do. Week after week, I went to church, but I had this question of whether God even loved me still. I thought, *If He loved me, wouldn't He have healed my mom?* I wrestled with all of those things.

I looked up everywhere I could find where the people in Scripture experienced a drought that led to famine, or a war that led to famine, or pestilence that led to famine, to see if I could find anything I could have used, or that you could use, or that I should have used, or maybe that I could have stumbled on. It took me a long time, and so I want to accelerate it for you to show you what these giants of the faith did to navigate these impossible, dry seasons of famine.

I'm starting here with David because I want you to see part of his story in 2 Samuel 21.

> **NOW THERE WAS A FAMINE IN THE DAYS OF DAVID FOR THREE YEARS, YEAR AFTER YEAR; AND DAVID INQUIRED OF THE LORD. AND THE LORD ANSWERED...**
>
> **—VERSE 1**

When you're going through a famine of your soul, like Amos mentioned, you're going to have to do something difficult. You're going to have to inquire of the Lord about your situation if you want an answer from the Lord about your situation. You may think that's obvious. Not so much. Many years ago in Ireland, there was a great famine that hit the Irish agricultural landscape. A massive famine hit the farmers. A tiny infestation began, and as it went unnoticed in this hidden component, it ultimately destroyed the crop. Many, many people died because of this small, hidden thing that went undetected. This is what I've found in my life: I must inquire of the Lord because there are small, hidden, undetected things that go on in my heart and soul that I don't even know are there until He highlights them for me in His Word and says, "Here's what's happening. And here are the steps you can take to change things."

I had to courageously examine my own soul, and so will you when you go through those dry seasons. You need to be open to God examining every secret component of your heart, every corner, every edge, every place He wants to go. Let him examine everything that's going on in your heart and mind. In other words, you cannot hold anything in reserve. If you're going to take this action step, you will say, "God, here's everything. It's all here. Here is everything that I have." This takes tremendous courage, because I don't know about you, but I'm a master at saying, "Hey, God, here's everything— except this one thing," thinking He doesn't know it exists. When I do that, I am lying to myself.

If you were to show up at my house today, I wouldn't be as hospitable as I could be. I would invite you in and ask you to sit down, and I would offer you something to drink. We would have a nice conversation, but if you ask for a tour, there are going to be some parts of the house you won't see. There are hidden parts of our homes that are reserved for me and my family alone, and they are the only ones on planet earth who know it exists.

The same is true in our hearts. We must fight through a lot

and courageously examine our souls. Socrates said it this way: "The unexamined life is not worth living." Psalm 77:6 (AMP) puts it this way:

> **I WILL REMEMBER MY SONG IN THE NIGHT; I WILL MEDITATE WITH MY HEART, AND MY SPIRIT SEARCHES.**

Psalm 119:59 (AMP) says this:

> **I CONSIDERED MY WAYS AND TURNED MY FEET TO [FOLLOW AND OBEY] YOUR TESTIMONIES.**

Finally, Lamentations 3:40 (NASB) says this:

> **LET US EXAMINE AND PROBE OUR WAYS, AND LET US RETURN TO THE LORD.**

Let's look at our hearts' limitations. The Bible doesn't say, "Why don't you examine everybody else's lives and find out what's wrong with them?" It tells us to examine *our* ways. We are to probe our ways like it's our full-time job. I've got a lot to manage in my own life. It's my job to examine and explore all of it. This self-reflection—the courageous self-examination of these things—involves looking at our own lives and returning to God. I was unwilling to do this, or I was unaware that I needed to do this. The heavens continued to *seem* closed because I pursued things other than what God wanted for my life, and those things did not get me out of the struggle in which I found myself.

I'm going to make a confession. When I was walking through this season, doing my best to lead my church, I was trapped by sin. Here's what it was. I had become accustomed to relying on Tylenol PM to self-medicate the emotional pain that was going on in my life. I'm not proud of that—actually, I'm pretty embarrassed about it—but when I was given the choice to pursue hope or to pursue sleep, I chose to pursue sleep. When I was asleep, it was the only time when I was oblivious to the world around me, and it was, for a moment, a counterfeit hope. Instead of examining my life, instead of going to God about the situation, what I did was to prioritize myself, my own interests, my own agenda, and my own way of thinking. I gave up on looking to God for assistance. I just took the medicine, hoping sleep would make it all disappear. But do you know what I found when I woke up? That thing was right there at the foot of my bed, waiting for me to wake up. I didn't advance. I stayed stuck. That's what sin does—it gets you stuck, and it keeps you stuck.

This is the thing that has become unfashionable to discuss in our culture, in our world, and in almost all of our churches. Sin has become the unfashionable thing to discuss. It's easier just to let it go. But let me tell you something. Sin is destructive.

Sin is a killer. Sin will rob you of everything that God wants you to experience in life. And let me tell you something else. Sin is not reserved only for people who don't know Jesus yet. Christians, Christ followers, have to deal with sin in our lives as well from time to time. Here's the truth: If you don't deal with sin, sin will deal with you. It'll keep you stuck where you are in your life.

What is sin? I love what the New Testament writer says in James 4:17 (NASB):

> **THEREFORE, TO ONE WHO KNOWS THE RIGHT THING TO DO AND DOES NOT DO IT, TO HIM IT IS SIN.**

If you know one way is the right way, but you choose a different way, that is sin. God doesn't label this "sin" because He's trying to deprive you of a good time or of something pleasurable, enjoyable, or fun. He labels something as sin because it's destructive, because it will destroy you, because it's not in your best interest. He labels it as "sin" so that you will stay away from it. Unless you think you have the power to get away from it yourself, you need to understand this truth. The cross of Christ has once and for all dealt with the sin problem, and Jesus did for you what you couldn't do for yourself. He took sin and nailed it to the cross, once and for all. He dominated sin for us so that we could live free from it. However, as long as we refuse to acknowledge that we have sin in our lives, it will have its way.

What did I do? Finally, after a period of time, I went to my wife. It was one of the hardest things I had to do, but I said, "Baby, I'm hooked on these pills." I didn't mean I was addicted. I meant I just wanted to sleep through the pain. Taking those pills was the only way I could get any peace. My wife lovingly, kindly, and mercifully said, "I will take those from you, and I will help you. We will get through this together."

We'll always be as sick as our secrets. And as long as they stay hidden, as long as they are still festering inside you, they have the potential to destroy you and God's plan for your life. But as soon as those things are revealed, as soon as you speak with someone, as soon as you give those sins back to God, as soon as you say, "I know Christ dealt with this and He gave me the power to overcome it," you bring it out as you courageously examine your own soul. You'll find that, even though it doesn't undo the past and the hurt and pain you experienced, a bit of refreshing will come back into your soul as you take one step at a time. When the heavens seem closed, His grace is still sufficient for you.

If you've ever had a down day, you know how it can pull the strength out of you. What I hope to do is add strength back into your life. Hard times will come to any person who has oxygen in their lungs. That is the single determining factor on when life will send you difficult things.

When my mom passed away, I had hopes and aspirations and confidence that the situation was going to turn around, but it didn't turn out the way I had expected. Many of us have written the script for our lives, and we say, "Hey, I think it'd be awesome if this, this, and this happened." But sometimes the brook dries up, and sometimes life gets dry. Sometimes life gets challenging. Sometimes the relationship is harder than we thought it was going to be. Sometimes the job situation doesn't pan out the way we thought it would. Sometimes our physical health is just not what we hoped it would be. The question then becomes, "What do I do when the brook dries up?" "What do I do when I have questions in life?" When my mom passed away, I didn't understand. We had been praying and believing for her situation to turn around, for a different outcome. But then 1 Corinthians 13 began to speak to me. Here's what Paul says:

> **WHEN I WAS A CHILD, I USED TO SPEAK LIKE A CHILD, THINK LIKE A CHILD, REASON LIKE A CHILD; WHEN I BECAME A MAN, I DID AWAY WITH CHILDISH THINGS.**
>
> **—1 CORINTHIANS 13:11 NASB**

Do you have children who are old enough to have outgrown some of their childish ways? Isn't it awesome when that happens? I have four kids, and there are nearly three years between the oldest and the youngest. I sometimes jokingly say that we had four children in less than three years because we had high energy and low IQ. We had four in diapers at one time! We had four kids needing the help of two adults. It was a messy situation. So, when the day came that they could wipe themselves, dress themselves, bathe themselves, and get themselves in a car, it was an amazing accomplishment for the Pennington household. It was awesome. Paul was saying that when you're a child, you do things that children do. As my children have grown, it's been one of the greatest joys of my life to watch them grow from the point that I'm feeding them to the point that I'm not only not feeding them, but they're making their own food. Then the day came when one of them made *me* a sandwich! It's a glorious thing when kids grow up! And when the child buys for the parent, that's amazing. Paul's talking about that. There's a growth process that happens in all of us.

When my mom died, the season of my life became dark, and I didn't know what to do. What I've learned is that when seasons are dark and dry, I retreat into a place in my mind that focuses on questions rather than answers. But eventually the day came when I matured and set aside my childish ways. I began to see the faint reflection of the riddles and mysteries, which life is full of. Paul says that one day we're going to see clearly, but right now my understanding is incomplete. One day I will understand everything, just as everything about me has been fully understood.

All of us have things that have happened in our lives; dark seasons, dry seasons. You might be going through one right now. Certainly, someone you know is walking through one of these dry seasons of life. The reason you need to know of their struggles is so that love can be your pursuit in helping them walk through and navigate that difficult season. I refuse to sit in judgment of anyone, except to judge them worthy of love. I hope you will choose that path as well.

Is unbelief real? Yes. Is it damaging and destructive? Yes. Is it our responsibility to trust God for things? Yes. I'm going to try to walk that tightrope of two converging worlds that seem to be in direct opposition to each other. I'm going to give you a definition for unbelief and for faith, and you're going to settle it once and for all. If you've ever wrestled with whether you are walking in unbelief or not, I'm going to make it very simple for you. Jesus Himself addressed the issue. Someone was in need of healing, and the disciples went to help that individual but they didn't get the outcome they were looking for. So, we find in Matthew 17:19:

> **THEN THE DISCIPLES CAME TO JESUS PRIVATELY AND SAID, "WHY COULD WE NOT CAST IT OUT?"**

In other words, why, Jesus, did we not get the same results that You had when You cast them out?

> **SO JESUS SAID TO THEM, "BECAUSE OF YOUR UNBELIEF."**
>
> **—VERSE 20**

You need to know to whom Jesus was talking here and what

He was talking about. Jesus was not talking to a sick person in this verse. He was talking to the disciples, who asked Him a very specific question. The reason I mention this is because if you isolate any one passage of Scripture and pull it out as a platform on which you build your beliefs and theology, you're in very dangerous territory. What's required is that all of the Scriptures have to agree in order to have appropriate biblical interpretation.

Here's what Jesus was saying to the disciples: "You didn't get the outcome you were looking for because you didn't believe it would work for *you*. You believed it would work for Me, not you." I want to give you a definition of unbelief. Unbelief is the active, ongoing abuse of, or blatant disregard for, the truth. If you're walking in unbelief, I have good news: There's a solution for it. Belief is the opposite. Belief is the ongoing process of confident expectation. It's living and active. If you are actively pursuing the truth, even if you don't know everything there is to know about the matter, you are still living in faith.

Jesus went on:

> **"ASSUREDLY, I SAY TO YOU, IF YOU HAVE FAITH AS A MUSTARD SEED, YOU WILL SAY TO THIS MOUNTAIN, 'MOVE FROM HERE TO THERE,' AND IT WILL MOVE; AND NOTHING WILL BE IMPOSSIBLE FOR YOU."**
>
> **—MATTHEW 17:20**

Here's the question: Do you accept what God has said about your life as the truth? If you have, then you have faith in your heart for that area in which you've accepted His truth. Where you're resisting, where you're blatantly disregarding, where you're rejecting and refusing to accept His truth, that's where unbelief rests. And that's the dangerous territory. So, faith is this. Faith is when my heart is focused on the greatness of my God, not the greatness of my outcomes. It's when I say, "God, You're bigger than the external circumstances that I see. God, I don't understand it, I have questions, but You're greater. I'm not going to reduce my faith to the level of what I can see and what I wish for and what I had hoped would happen. I'm not going to lower my standard of how great You are based on how terrible this one life moment has been, because You never change—You're good yesterday, today, and tomorrow, and You're not going to change. You never have. You never will. In fact, God, You're greater than I even realize You are. You're better than I thought You were. You are bigger than anything I could ever face. So, I'm not going to change, either."

The world may not get it. The world may not understand it. It may tell you to give up on God, give up on your faith, and go a different direction. But no matter what the outcome is, the greatness of God never changes. Don't build your faith on a specified, desired outcome; build your faith on something deeper, something stronger, something with a better foundation, which is Jesus Christ—the One who will never change, the One who will never leave you, the One who will never forsake you.

I want a faith that will stand in the good times and the bad times. I want a faith that will stand when the sun is shining and when the rain is pouring. I want a faith that lives in my heart and says, "I don't care what the outcome is, I'm going with God's plan for my life because His plan is better than what anybody else could ever come up with. He's the only One who sent His Son to die for me so that I can live. I'm going to build my life on that." Get your mind off of you and your issues and get your mind back on the greatness of your God, because He's the One who got you from where you were to where you are. And He's the One who is going to get you from where you are to where you need to be. Because of Christ, there's hope, even when the heavens seem closed.

You have a decision to make. Are you going to follow Him? Even when you don't understand? Can you submit what you are going through to Him? It's in the moments when you don't understand that truth actually has an opportunity to erupt in your heart. When you know, you know. You don't need faith for the things you know, because you have sight. You need faith for the things you can't see. We walk by faith, not by sight. Here's what God promises in Psalm 37:19 (NLT):

> **THEY WILL NOT BE DISGRACED IN HARD TIMES; EVEN IN FAMINE THEY WILL HAVE MORE THAN ENOUGH.**

And He says this in Isaiah 58:11:

THE LORD WILL GUIDE YOU CONTINUALLY, AND SATISFY YOUR SOUL IN DROUGHT, AND STRENGTHEN YOUR BONES; YOU SHALL BE LIKE A WATERED GARDEN, AND LIKE A SPRING OF WATER, WHOSE WATERS DO NOT FAIL.

We are not designed to perish. His will for us is that we would all inherit eternal life. I need you to know this: Heaven is real. Hell is real. Today you can make a decision that will cause you to know that heaven will be your forever home. Jesus said that He is the way, the truth, and the life. Nobody gets to the Father except through Him. He made a way of escape for us. He made a way forward for us. If you don't know Him, decide to make him the Lord of your life today; make Him the center of your world. If you know what it means to know Him, and He has not been the center of your life, I'm asking you to make a change today and come back home to God.

AFTERWORD

I don't want to conclude this book without first talking to you about heaven. **You can *know* you are going to heaven when you die!**

From my earliest childhood, I attended church. The challenge for me, however, was that I met the Church before I met Jesus. Although I believe deeply in the power of the local church, going to church doesn't save *anyone*. I didn't meet *Jesus* until the church I grew up in presented a drama that introduced me to Him. At that young age, I was confronted with the reality of eternity, and I decided I wanted to spend forever *with* Jesus, *not* separated from Him. That night the play I witnessed quite literally scared hell right out of me!

That night I accepted Jesus as my Lord and Savior, and from that moment on, I have had the deep assurance that I will spend eternity with God in heaven.

Let me ask you a few questions.

Do you know for certain where you will spend eternity? Will it be in heaven?

What would you say if God were to ask you when you die, "Why should I let you into My heaven?"

If you are unsure of what you would say, or if you hesitate for even a moment in answering these questions, the next few paragraphs of this book can make all the difference to your future!

God says this in His Word:

> **THESE THINGS I HAVE WRITTEN TO YOU WHO BELIEVE IN THE NAME OF THE SON OF GOD, THAT YOU MAY KNOW THAT YOU HAVE ETERNAL LIFE....**
>
> **—1 JOHN 5:13**

How can we know that we have eternal life?

Heaven is a free gift! The Bible tells us, "The gift of God is eternal life in Christ Jesus our Lord" (Romans 6:23).

This is good news! A true gift is freely given and freely received. In this case, eternal life is freely given by God, and this gift can be freely received by us or anyone—no matter who you are or what you've done. Heaven is not earned or deserved by us, because everyone sins:

> **ALL HAVE SINNED AND FALL SHORT**
> **OF THE GLORY OF GOD.**
>
> **—ROMANS 3:23**

Sin is the breaking of God's Law, and includes lying, cheating, deceit, stealing, evil thoughts, and immoral behavior, among other things. Have you ever wondered just how good you would have to be to make it to heaven? Because it is impossible to be perfect, even the smallest sin disqualifies us from heaven. We can't be good enough to get in, so there must be an entirely different way to be admitted to heaven! God is merciful, and He does not want to punish us. He says this:

> **YES, I HAVE LOVED YOU WITH AN EVERLASTING LOVE.**
>
> **—JEREMIAH 31:3**

The same Bible that tells us God loves us also tells us that God is perfectly just. So, He must punish sin. He is "by no means clearing the guilty" (Exodus 34:7). God solved this problem in the Person of Jesus Christ.

Who would you say Jesus is? The Bible teaches that Jesus is God. Anyone who wants to know what God is like can find out from the perfect and sinless life of Jesus. He died on the cross and rose from the dead to pay the penalty for our sins and to purchase a place for us in heaven, which He offers as a free gift. God loved us so much that He gave the only thing He has one of: His Son, Jesus.

Does everyone receive this gift? No. This gift is received by faith. Faith is the key that opens the door to eternal life in heaven. It is not a blind leap in the dark. It is not just head knowledge. Nor is it just a temporary belief. Saving faith means trusting in Jesus Christ alone as one's Rescuer and Giver of eternal life. It means believing in Jesus alone, and on what He has done, rather than anything we can do for ourselves to gain heaven.

> **FOR GOD SO LOVED THE WORLD THAT HE GAVE HIS ONLY BEGOTTEN SON, THAT WHOEVER BELIEVES IN HIM SHOULD NOT PERISH BUT HAVE ETERNAL LIFE.**
>
> **—JOHN 3:16**

Would you like to receive God's gift of eternal life? Because this is so important, let's clarify what it involves.

TRUST HIM

This means you accept Christ as your Savior. Open the "door" to your life and invite Him in. He says this:

> **BEHOLD, I STAND AT THE DOOR AND KNOCK. IF ANYONE HEARS MY VOICE AND OPENS THE DOOR, I WILL COME IN TO HIM.**
>
> **—REVELATION 3:20**

This means you also must receive Him as the Lord of your life, giving Him the driver's seat in your life, not the back seat. It means that you need to repent—that is, be willing to turn away from anything that is not pleasing to God. He will tell you what He wants you to do as you grow in your relationship with Him, and He will give you the strength to do it. You can receive this gift of eternal life through Jesus Christ, right where you are.

FOR WITH THE HEART ONE BELIEVES UNTO RIGHTEOUSNESS, AND WITH THE MOUTH CONFESSION IS MADE UNTO SALVATION.

—ROMANS 10:10

You can pray right now and receive eternal life. Pray the following prayer out loud:

DEAR HEAVENLY FATHER, THANK YOU FOR YOUR SON, JESUS. I ACCEPT THAT HE LIVED A PERFECT LIFE, WAS CRUCIFIED IN MY PLACE, AND WAS RAISED FROM THE DEAD. I BELIEVE IN MY HEART AND I SPEAK IT OUT LOUD WITH MY MOUTH: JESUS IS LORD. I TURN FROM SIN, AND I TURN TO YOUR SON INSTEAD. I WILL FOLLOW HIM ALL THE DAYS OF MY LIFE. AMEN.

If this prayer expresses what you believe in your heart, Jesus promises you this: *You may know that you have eternal life!* If you have truly turned away from your sins, placed your trust in Jesus Christ's sacrificial death, and received the gift of eternal life, you are now a child of God! Forever!

> **AS MANY AS RECEIVED HIM, TO THEM HE GAVE THE RIGHT TO BECOME CHILDREN OF GOD, TO THOSE WHO BELIEVE IN HIS NAME.**
>
> **—JOHN 1:12**

You can now be sure you are *going to heaven!* Welcome to God's family! So, what's next?

I would love to point you toward your next step in beginning your walk with God by completing the Five Habits of Spiritual Growth course. This course will lead your through five important components that will help you to grow spiritually and learn to be a self feeder. Here is what you will learn in the Five Habits course.

HABIT 1 *THE WORD*
7 WAYS TO LEARN FROM THE WORD OF GOD

HABIT 2 *PRAYER*
KEYS TO A SUCCESSFUL PRAYER LIFE

HABIT 3 *LIVING A SPIRIT-LED LIFE*
GETTING TO KNOW THE HOLY SPIRIT

HABIT 4 *WORSHIP*
TRUTHS ABOUT WORSHIP

Worship allows us to rely on God's power to steer us through life. Whereas, stress and worry are residual effects of relying on yourself and being your own god. Something remarkable happens when you worship, you step into a new way of life. Worship opens up another world to you and here is what the enemy hates about it.

HABIT 5 *GIVING*

- THREE AREAS OF GIVING
- BENEFITS OF GIVING
- REASONS WHY WE GIVE

To access all of this content in its entirety go to:

joshpennington.org/five-habits

Made in United States
Orlando, FL
07 July 2023

34830457R00080